AS GOOD AS GOLD
HISTORY OF THE POUND STERLING

Ian Moncrief-Scott

Information Management Solutions Limited

ISLE OF MAN

The author Ian Moncrief-Scott has asserted his right under the Copyright, Designs and Patents Act 1988 to be identified as the author of this work.

Copyright. © I. Moncrief-Scott 2021

All rights reserved. No part of this publication may be produced in any form or by any means - graphic, electronic, or mechanical, including photocopying, recording, taping, or information storage and retrieval systems - without the prior permission in writing of the publishers.

The publishers make no representation, express or implied, regarding the accuracy of the information contained in this book and cannot accept any legal responsibility for any errors or omissions that may take place.

A CIP catalogue record for this book is available from the British Library.

Published by Information Management Solutions Limited, 17 Howe Road, Onchan, Isle of Man, IM3 2BB.

Printed, bound and distributed by IngramSpark.

Book Layout © 2017 BookDesignTemplates.com

Superhero Peg Image: Besjunior/Shutterstock.com

Cover Source by Tanja Prokop of BookDesignTemplates.com

AS GOOD AS GOLD: HISTORY OF THE POUND STERLING – 2nd ed.
ISBN 99781903467039

The Publishers have been requested by the author to acknowledge the direct and indirect contributions to this book by:

The Bank of England
Mr David Sinclair
Daily Mail Newspapers

This book is dedicated to
start-up entrepreneurs.

The front cover depicts
ordinary wooden clothes pegs dressed as
Super Heroes.

**All start-up entrepreneurs are
ordinary people
turning into Super Heroes!**

CONTENTS

AS GOOD AS GOLD 1
BIBLIOGRAPHY 13
OTHER BOOKS BY THE AUTHOR 15
FORTHCOMING BOOKS BY THE AUTHOR 16

AS GOOD AS GOLD

Dwarfing the first heartbeats of the infant Euro, England's Pound spans almost an entire millennium.

Even the mighty US Dollar and the vanishing Franc, Mark and Lira can only muster 800 years between them.

Sterling's continuity and prosperity can largely be attributed to three leaders, King Henry VII, Queen Elizabeth I and Lady Margaret Thatcher.

Many have tried to destroy the currency.

Ten centuries ago, the English name 'pound' first appeared. Rooted to Roman Latin, 'pondus' meant 'a weight'. Despite weights devolving into uncla (ounce) and libra (pound) the term survived. Libra's first letter spawned the £ sign.

Pennies created by King Offa of Mercia, an 8th-century monarch better known for his Dyke, would ultimately inspire the Pound.

Nearly 500 years would pass before it would become a gold coin.

Peasants needed little cash. Eggs could be exchanged for Barley. Turnips swapped for milk. Cloth for wood. Barter prevailed.

In rare cases, if cash was essential, a corner could be sliced off a penny. Only wealthy merchants, landowners and the monarchy used money.

When the Vikings discovered Britain's rich lands, money was needed to pay them or repel their advances. A larger unit than a penny became inevitable.

King Alfred's records first mention the Pound.

His grandson, King Athelstan ordered a single national currency, the first in Europe since the Romans.

Even when William the Conqueror vanquished King Harold in 1066 the currency was so well respected that it survived. It supported the Norman's Domesday Book, a thorough register of the nation's assets.

Ordericus Vitalis, a 12-century monk recording Church history wrote the words 'libra sterilensum'. The Pound Sterling was born. Some contend the word emanates from 'esterlin', little star, evident on Norman pennies, which appears in early text as 'starlings'.

In 1108, William's son, King Henry I, decreed that any purveyor of debased silver pennies should be 'castrated and his eyes put out'. Early English silver coins were virtually pure silver, but fraudulent 'skimming and clipping' was increasingly commonplace.

While halving and quartering were routine, deliberate devaluation became a serious crime.

Widespread belief that many silver coins were minted with base metals, to lower production costs and cheat the unwary, convinced people to 'check' coins with cuts and scrapes. Four years later, the resolute monarch decreed that a groove should be cut across the coin's face to prove its content.

Still, the problems continued.

In 1124, the King summoned leading minters. Determined to cease the debased silver pennies, he called them to trial.

Over that Christmas at Winchester, more than one hundred men were separated from their hands and genitalia. They were taken 'one by one and deprived each of the right hand and the testicles beneath', according to documents of the day.

Sadly, little improvement transpired.

In 1279, Edward I initiated strict silver regulations for pennies and introduced farthings (1/4 pennies) and the next year, halfpennies.

As the economy grew, silver groats, worth four pence, arrived to bolster the higher denominations of the shilling, mark and pound.

By 1344, came the 'florin', worth six shillings or 72 pennies and, in 1412, the 'noble' would realise 80 pennies. 1465 witnessed the issue of gold 'ryals' at ten shillings or half a pound.

Foreign coins also gained acceptance to meet the growing shortage of English currency.

An inconspicuous Leicestershire hillside, Bosworth Field, provided the venue for a clash between two mighty medieval armies in 1485. Young Henry Tudor's decisive victory over Richard III ceased years of civil war and sparked economic stability.

Within three years, Henry VII issued the first gold pound coin. Designed by a German, Alexander de Bruchsal, the piece was magnificent – heavy, pure gold.

He encouraged the issue of the gold sovereign and the shilling. Cash usage was further facilitated by denominations of the groat, half groat and penny to the silver angel (1/3 Pound) and ryal (1/2 Pound).

15th century England saw its coinage reported as the 'envy of Europe for its fineness, handsomeness and execution.'

His successor, Henry VIII was not so kind to the currency.

Even vast wealth pillaged from monasteries and churches could not satisfy his lust for war and supplement his lavish court lifestyle.

Soon, the coinage lost its reputation.

New coins were minted in Ireland. These 'harps' paid the soldiers but quickly circulated in England. The Great Debasement continued. Foreign merchants refused English money.

In less than fifty years, his father's great achievement was shattered.

Help was to hand. Queen Elizabeth I, the late King's daughter withdrew the debased money and reissued coins of standard gold and silver measure. Aided by brave and resourceful mariners like Sir Francis Drake, she redressed the balance.

Some historians argue it was little more than state piracy.

In reality, England was a long-term enemy of Spain. These commissioned privateers were authorised to seize foreign treasure at will. Millions poured into the coffers in silver, jewels, art and gold. The value of the pound was again restored.

Throughout the 18th century gold slowly evolved as the underlying choice for coins of high value.

In 1816, Parliament passed The Coinage Act to establish a formal currency system and create the first gold sovereign.

Soon banknotes emerged. These, backed by gold reserves led to the 'Gold Standard.' Britain's banknotes were 'as good as gold' which underpinned her overwhelming economic and monetary superiority.

Unlike earlier wars, which had actually helped the Pound, the First World War generated economic chaos. For the first time in centuries, war challenged the Pound's indomitable position.

In 1933, Britain was forced to drop The Gold Standard. The USA seized firm industrial control to catapult the Dollar as the pre-eminent international currency.

The Second World War only added to the Pound's misery.

Closer European ties in 1971 saw Decimalisation herald an end to tradition with the death of 20 Shillings and 240 Pence to the Pound.

During the 1980s, Lady Margaret Thatcher brilliantly transformed Britain's sick industrial base to restore the respect, trust and confidence the Pound enjoys today.

No longer gold, today's coin is a blend of copper, zinc and nickel weighing a mere 9.5 grams. Will it endure?

Or, as history reveals, will another weak and indulgent custodian write a final chapter?

BIBLIOGRAPHY

Clapham, J. (1944). *The Bank of England a History*. Cambridge: Cambridge University Press.

Moncrief-Scott, I. (2000). *The Eternal Old Lady - Bank of England - History & Development.* York: Appleton.

Richards, R.D. (1934) *The First 50 Years of The Bank of England (1694–1744).* Leiden: Nijhoff.

Saw, R. (1944). *The Bank of England* 1694-1944. London: Harrap.

OTHER BOOKS BY THE AUTHOR

As Good As Gold - History of Pound Sterling. ISBN 0-9534818-4-0

De La Rue Straw Hats to Global Securities. ISBN 0- 9534818-2-4

Euro History & Development. ISBN 0-9534818-1-6

Holidays 2000 – A Time Capsule. ISBN 0-9534818-7-5

Negotiate to Win! - The Introductory Edition. ISBN 0-9534818-6-7

Start Any Business (Print). ISBN 9781903467008
Start Any Business (eBook). ISBN 9781903467015

Scripophily - Historic Bond & Share Collecting. ISBN 0-9534818-5-9

The Eternal Old Lady - Bank of England. ISBN 0-9534818-3-2

The Green Shoots of Money (Print). ISBN 9781903467107
The Green Shoots of Money (eBook). ISBN 9781903467114

The Hitmen - Part One. ISBN 0-9534818-8-3

FORTHCOMING BOOKS BY THE AUTHOR

As Good As Gold (Print). ISBN 9781903467039
As Good As Gold (eBook). ISBN 9781903467121

Currants, Olives & Cotton (Print). ISBN 9781903467077
Currants, Olives & Cotton (eBook). ISBN 9781903467169

De La Rue (Print). ISBN 9781903467046
De La Rue (eBook). ISBN 9781903467138

Euro (Print). ISBN 9781903467053
Euro (eBook). ISBN 9781903467145

Scripophily (Print). ISBN 9781903467084
Scripophily (eBook). ISBN 9781903467176

Tail-less Cats & Three-legged Men (Print). ISBN 9781903467091
Tail-less Cats & Three-legged Men (eBook). ISBN 9781903467183

The Eternal Old Lady (Print). ISBN 9781903467060
The Eternal Old Lady (eBook). ISBN 9781903467152

ABOUT THE AUTHOR

Ian Moncrief-Scott has over fifty years of broad business experience, mostly gained at international level, based in the UK.

As a former senior executive for a global publishing and information technology company headquartered in the USA, he has contributed to numerous client-facing procurement and outsourcing initiatives worldwide.

Ian has created and participated in numerous small businesses in the UK, Isle of Man and elsewhere.

He has also represented the Isle of Man Government Department for Enterprise in several of its business support schemes. Ian designed and delivered extensive training for its Micro Business Grant Scheme.

In recognition of his long-term service to the Department, Ian was nominated for The Queen's Award for Enterprise Promotion and awarded an official Certificate of Recognition in 2018.

Throughout his career, he has maintained an active interest in start-ups, especially those involving the financial sector.

At the turn of the millennium, several of the articles written by Ian that form this short work were originally published by the Museum of American Financial History (now the Museum of American Finance).

www.ingramcontent.com/pod-product-compliance
Lightning Source LLC
Chambersburg PA
CBHW071722080526
44588CB00012B/1871